Donald's Guide to Robert's Rules

Written by: Donald Garrett

Donald Garrett
Visit my website at www.DonaldGarrett.com

Printed in the United States of America

First Printing: November 2010

Edited by Paulette Whitehurst

ISBN-13: 978-1453701430

To my family-
My biological one and my TSA one

TABLE OF CONTENTS

1
The Basics

So by now you're probably thinking "What is parliamentary procedure, and why do I need it?" or "Who is Robert, and why did he make rules?" and "Do I really have to read through that 704-paged book?" Well, hopefully since you bought this pocket guide, you trust me enough to help you learn about Robert's Rules of Order in a quick, efficient manner. In this chapter, we will study the fundamentals of parliamentary law, the rights of members, and other basic things to give you a great foundation for the rest of this guide. Using parliamentary procedure in your club, society, organization, or other association will be beneficial because it gives members a standard set of rules to help expedite business. Studying parliamentary procedure can be challenging at times but the end result is rewarding.

What is parliamentary procedure?

Parliamentary procedure or **parliamentary law** is a set of rules, customs, and ethics that guide the governance of clubs, organizations, and other deliberative bodies. It allows a deliberative body to reach a group decision through self-governance and debate. Parliamentary procedure originated in the UK with the British House of Commons. Their rules on how to pass bills found its way all around the world.

Who uses parliamentary procedure?

A **deliberative body** is a group of people that use parliamentary procedure to make decisions. These groups are made of people who have the freedom to meet and discuss courses of action to be taken in the name of the entire body.

Who is Robert, and what is his story?

Henry M. Robert was a brigadier general in the US Army in the late 1800's. One day, he was asked to lead a business meeting at his church. His performance was so poor that he vowed to not attend another church meeting until he studied parliamentary procedure. Thus, the *Pocket Manual of Rules of Order for Deliberative Assemblies* was born. Robert used his research to lead a subsequent church meeting. His manual was so successful that it found its way around the world. Ten editions (as of June 2010) have been printed, and average organizations use it every day to run their business meetings quickly and efficiently.

Do I have to read through that 704-paged book?

The answer is yes and no. It all depends on you and how much you want to study parliamentary procedure. It is the intent of this guide to give you a great foundation on parliamentary procedure so that you can tackle the big book with ease or just so you can understand what's happening at your organization's next business meeting.

Types of Deliberative Bodies

Now that we know who generally uses parliamentary procedure, it's time to add subdivisions to the broad term "deliberative body." The 5 types of deliberative bodies are:

- Mass meetings
- Local chapters of an organized society
- Conventions
- Legislative bodies
- Boards

Mass Meetings are large assemblies of people. It is the meeting of an unorganized group that is announced open to the general public interested in a certain problem. They meet and decide on appropriate action to address the issue. Examples include: People who are opposed to a recent tax increase and members of a neighborhood who want to address an issue facing all residents.

Local Chapters of an organized society are groups of people who belong to a bigger parent organization who wish to meet on a more frequent basis with other members who live geographically close to each other.

Conventions are an assembly of delegates who are representatives from constituent local chapters.

The delegates from the different chapters meet in order to take action on behalf of the larger state or national society.

Legislative bodies are constitutionally mandated lawmaking bodies for the general public. Examples include: Congress, state legislatures, and local city councils.

Boards are an administrative body of elected or appointed people. They set policy and act on behalf of the general membership. Examples include: the board of visitors for a public university that is appointed by a state governor or the board of trustees for a stock corporation that is elected annually by the shareholders.

Rules

Organizations get their rules of operation from various sources. These rules set basic structure and manner of operation.

A **Corporate Charter**, also called **Articles of Incorporation**, is a legal document that gives the name and object of an association. Different states have rules involving incorporation. It is suggested that your organization has a corporate charter if it wishes to hold property; inherit a legacy; make legally binding contracts; hire employees; be in a position to sue or be sued; and protect the members from personal liability. A corporate charter should be drafted by an attorney and submitted in accordance with your state's laws.

The **Constitution** and/or **Bylaws** of an organization are documents that contain the organization's basic rules. They describe the characteristics of the organization and how it should function. They also have provisions related to members, officers, committees, and other procedures unique to the organization.

Rules of Order are the set of parliamentary procedures that an organization adopts. These rules deal with the transaction of business and offer an efficient way for members to be involved in self-governance.

Standing Rules are additions to the rules of order the organization has already adopted. They provide for miscellaneous things that are necessary to handle the business of the organization. An example of a standing rule is a rule setting the hour for beginning the meetings.

Your Rights

Standard members of deliberative bodies have the same rights. Some organizations, however; do have different classes of membership that spread the standard rights out among different ranks. The six basic rights of members are:

- to attend meetings
- to make motions
- to debate motions
- to nominate
- to vote
- to hold office

All standard members of the organization should have equal rights. The presiding officer should give equal protection of these rights to all members (unless the organization's constitution and/or bylaws divide the rights up among different classes of members).

One Thing at a Time

Only one question can be considered at a time. This helps decrease confusion amongst the members of the deliberative body. Also, one person may debate at a time. Once a member has been *"yielded the floor,"* or recognized to speak, he cannot be interrupted by another speaker except in very rare cases.

2
Business

Deliberative bodies, in any form, meet to do one thing, transact business. The use of parliamentary procedure allows for the easy transaction of business. There are, however, some basic requirements that must occur for the body to begin discussion. There also needs to be a pattern of respect to insure that no member's feelings are hurt during the course of business.

Quorum

A **quorum**, simply stated, is the minimum number of people that must be present in order for business to be transacted. This is normally set in an organization's constitution or bylaws. In the case of a board or a committee, it is usually a majority. The purpose of a quorum is to make sure that there is a big enough group authorizing decisions on behalf of the whole body. If a quorum is not present, business cannot take place.

Basic Officers

Every deliberative body needs at least two officers to operate: a presiding officer and a secretary. The **presiding officer** (also known as a **chairman** or **president**) keeps the order of the meeting. He conducts the meeting and makes sure the rules are being observed. While presiding, he is referred to as *"the chair."* The **secretary** (also known as a **clerk** or **scribe**) writes minutes. **Minutes** are a record of what business was transacted at the meeting.

The Consideration of a Motion

This is where we begin to delve into the world of parliamentary procedure. A **motion** is a proposal. All motions require a second. A person other than the maker of the motion *seconds* the motion when he agrees that it should be *brought before the assembly.*

A **main motion** is a motion that brings business before the deliberative body. The maker of the motion begins his proposal with "I move to..." or "I move that..." Motions must <u>always</u> be made in the affirmative. It is <u>wrong</u> to say "I move to not..." or "I move that we don't..."

In order to introduce his proposal, the maker must receive recognition from the presiding officer. This is done by rising up and saying "Mr. President" or the title the deliberative body gives its presiding officer. The officer will then recognize the individual by stating his name, if possible.

Mr. A: [*Rises*] Mr. President

Chair: Mr. A

Mr. A: I move to build a playground in the neighborhood.

At this point, the motion needs a second in order to receive consideration in the deliberative body. The person who agrees the motion should be considered, or the **seconder**, should say "I second the motion" or "I second it" or yell "Second!" This is done without obtaining the floor. The seconder can second a motion from his seat. However, in larger bodies it is recommended that the seconder rise to second the motion.

The presiding officer, hearing the motion and its second, should then restate the motion. Stating the motion opens the motion up for everyone at the meeting to consider. This is done by saying "It is moved is seconded [the motion]." If the motion did not receive a second, it dies.

Chair: It is moved and seconded to build a playground in the neighborhood.

OR

Chair: There is no second so the motion dies.

The motion is then open for debate. Immediately after stating the motion, the presiding officer should look to the maker of the motion. The maker of the motion has the right to debate first. There are a few things to observe during the debate of a motion:

- The maker of the motion has the right to speak first.

- No one should speak twice unless everyone who wants to debate has had their chance.

- The presiding officer should try to alternate between speakers who are for the motion and speakers who are against the motion.

- Personal attacks are <u>never</u> allowed. The presiding officer will call you out of order.

- Debate should stay on the current motion and not venture off onto other topics.

When the presiding officer recognizes you for debate, it is called *yielding the floor*. To obtain the floor, a member rises and says "Mr. President" or the title of the presiding officer. They then are recognized for debate. If two or more members rise, the presiding officer picks the one that rose first.

Mr. A: I believe we need to build this playground in order to give the children in our neighborhood a place to play.

Ms. B: [*Rises*] Mr. President

Chair: Ms. B

Ms. B: We already have other community planning projects going on so I'm not sure if there's enough room for the playground. Let's defeat this motion until a study can show where to place the playground.

Dr. C: (*Outbursts*) You're just another heartless person who doesn't care about the kids!

Chair: Dr. C, you are out of order please be seated. You may continue, Ms. B.

After the debate has concluded, it is time for the presiding officer to *put the question*. **Putting the question** is when the presiding officer ends debate and puts the motion up for a vote. Before he puts the question, the officer asks, "Are you ready for the question?" If no one asks to speak, it is time to vote. The chair says, "The question is on the motion [the text of the motion]."

> **Chair:** Are you ready for the question? (*Silence*) The question is on the motion to build a playground in the neighborhood.

After the presiding officer puts the question, it is time to vote. Main motions require a majority vote. A **majority vote** is more than half of the votes cast. Most motions require a majority vote. For example, if there were 100 votes cast, the majority (more than 50) is 51. If 15 votes were cast, the majority (more than 7.5) is 8. If a motion has a tie vote, it fails because those in favor did not receive more than half of the votes.

The most common method of voting is a voice vote. **Voice votes** (also known as **viva voce** or **acclamation**) occur when the presiding officer asks those in favor of the motion to say "aye" and those opposed to the motion to say "no." The louder side wins. At the conclusion of the vote, the presiding officer announces the winning side.

> **Chair:** All those in favor of the motion say "aye."
>
> **Some:** Aye
>
> **Chair:** All those opposed, say "no."
>
> **Some:** No
>
> **Chair:** The ayes have it and the motion is agreed to.
>
> OR
>
> **Chair:** The noes have it and the motion fails.

Some motions require a 2/3 vote. A **2/3 vote**

means at least two-thirds of the votes cast. For example, if 60 votes were cast, a 2/3 vote (at least 40) is 40 votes. If 61 votes were cast, a 2/3 vote (at least 40.66667) is 41 votes.

A **rising vote** occurs when the presiding officer asks for each side to rise when called upon. This provides for a more accurate account of how many people are for or against the motion. Motions requiring a 2/3 vote are always conducted by a standing vote.

> **Chair:** All those in favor of the motion please rise. [*Counts the number of people*] Thank you, be seated. All those opposed to the motion please rise. [*Counts the number of people*] Thank you, be seated. The ayes have it and the motion is agreed to.
>
> OR
>
> **Chair:** The noes have it and the motion fails.

Voting and related procedures will be discussed more and chapter 12.

Order of Business

The **order of business** is the sequence of which business should be taken up. Some deliberative bodies adopt their own order of business. Robert's Rules of Order recommends the following standard order of business:

I. Reading and Approval of Minutes

II. Reports from Officers, Boards, and Standing Committees

III. Reports from Special Committees

IV. Special Orders

V. Unfinished Business and General Orders

VI. New Business

Items I-IV will be discussed later on in this guide. During new business, members offer main motions as prescribed in this chapter.

No Quorum?

Sometimes meetings may not have enough people to transact business. If a quorum isn't present, the only motions in order are motions to recess, adjourn, set a special meeting date, or take measures to establish a quorum. The last type of motion includes a motion "to call absent members."

3
Subsidiary Motions

In Chapter 2 we learned about main motions. However, there are motions that can be made while the main motion is pending. A **secondary motion** relates to a main motion by procedural or emergency qualities. These motions are made during the debate of a main motion. When a secondary motion is placed before the assembly, it becomes the *immediate pending question.* It is disposed of before the final consideration of the main motion. There are 3 types of secondary motions: subsidiary, privileged, and incidental.

Subsidiary motions are motions that help dispose of a main motion. They include the motions to: postpone indefinitely; amend; commit; postpone to a certain time; limit or extend debate; the previous question; and lay on the table.

Postpone Indefinitely

The motion to postpone indefinitely stops further consideration of the motion to which it is applied. Simply stated, it "kills" the current motion.   Some characteristics of the motion are:

- It can only be applied to a main motion and requires a second.

- It is debatable and debate can extend to the main motion to which it is applied.

- It is *not* amendable.

- It requires a majority vote for adoption.

This motion is useful if it is important to not have a direct vote on a motion. For example, let's pretend a local chapter is considering a motion "to endorse the society's state president for his US House of Representatives campaign." Voting for the motion shows support for a fellow society member but members might have different political opinions.   Voting against the motion would make you seem like you're not a loyal member to the society.   This is where the motion to postpone indefinitely comes in play.

Mr. A: I move that the motion be postponed indefinitely.

Ms. B: Second!

Chair: It's been moved and seconded that the motion relating to the endorsement of the Society's State President be postponed indefinitely.

After debating the motion to postpone indefinitely, the chair puts the question. Depending on the voting results, the presiding officer announces to the assembly what action has been taken. If the motion to postpone indefinitely passes, the main motion dies; if it fails, debate on the main motion continues.

Chair: The ayes have it and the main motion is

postponed indefinitely.

OR

Chair: The noes have it and the motion to postpone fails. The question is on the motion to endorse the President. Is there any debate?

Amend

The motion to amend changes the wording of a pending motion. This motion *inserts, strikes out,* or *substitutes* the text of a motion. It is one of the most frequently used motions, because it allows the deliberative body to perfect the wording of a pending motion. Some characteristics of the motion are:

- It requires a second.
- It is debatable.
- It is amendable.
- It requires a majority vote for adoption.

The motion to amend can be applied to words, phrases, and paragraphs. For the following examples, a local community foundation is considering a motion "to host a fundraiser this summer."

Mr. A is in favor of the motion. However, he believes it's not specific enough. He can use a motion to amend in order to perfect the wording.

Mr. A: I move to amend the motion by inserting "bake sale" before "fundraiser."

In that example, Mr. A wanted to add clarification to what type of fundraiser the foundation was going to hold. Ms. B is in favor of having a fundraiser; however, she believes that since the summer is coming up, there wouldn't be enough time to plan the fundraiser.

> **Ms. B:** I move to amend the motion by striking out "this summer."

The two above uses of the motion to amend can also be combined. This is substituting text. Dr. C also agrees that there should be a fundraiser but he thinks that hosting a fundraiser would take too much time planning and that the foundation should join an already established fundraiser.

> **Dr. C:** I move to amend the motion by striking out "host" and inserting "join."

Motions to amend must be **germane**, or relate to the pending motion in some way. An amendment cannot be a disguise for new business. Motions that aren't germane should be ruled out of order by the presiding officer.

The first example was germane, because it related to the type of fundraiser the foundation was to take part of. The second example related to when the fundraiser was to take place. The third was germane, because it related to how the foundation was going to participate in a fundraiser (hosting or joining an already established one). The following is an example of an amendment that is not germane:

> **Rev. D:** I move to amend the motion by inserting "and pay the delegate's expenses for the upcoming convention."

> **Chair:** I'm sorry but that amendment is not germane. The pending motion relates to hosting a fundraiser. The amendment is out of order. Is there any more debate?

As stated previously, the motion to amend is amendable. When this motion is amending another motion, it's called a **primary amendment**. When the motion to amend is amending an amendment, it called a **secondary amendment**.

Let's look at Mr. A's motion to "amend the motion by inserting 'bake sale' before 'fundraiser.'" Mrs. E is allergic to some common ingredients in bake sale items.

> **Mrs. E:** I move to amend the amendment by inserting "gluten-free" before "bake sale." (*Second*)

The presiding officer has to be careful and always restate the amendments so that the entire assembly knows which motion is being considered. The pending motion, primary amendment, and secondary amendment should be disposed in the following order:

Main motion made → Primary amendment made → Secondary amendment made → Vote on secondary amendment → Vote on primary amendment → Vote on main motion

> **Chair:** It's been moved and seconded to amend the amendment by inserting "gluten-free" before "bake sale." If this secondary amendment is adopted, the primary amendment will read "gluten-free bake sale." The question is on inserting "gluten-free." Is there any debate? Mrs. E
>
> **Mrs. E:** Mr. President, I am allergic to common ingredients in baked goods. This amendment will allow people with food allergies to still purchase from the bakesale.
>
> **Dr. C:** [*Rises*] Mr. President
>
> **Chair:** Dr. C

Dr. C: This amendment limits the bake sale to only selling gluten-free goods. There should still be other options for those who are able to eat food with gluten and other ingredients.

Chair: Is there any more debate? Are you ready for the question? (*Silence*) The question is on the secondary amendment to insert "gluten free" before "bake sale." If adopted, the primary amendment will read "gluten-free bake sale." All those in favor please say "aye."

Some: Aye

Chair: All those opposed please say "no."

Some: No

Chair: The noes have it, and the amendment fails. The question is on the primary amendment to insert "bake sale" before "fundraiser."

At this point, debate on inserting "bake sale" before "fundraiser" occurs. Then the presiding officer puts the question.

Chair: Is there any more debate? Are you ready for the question? (*Silence*) The question is on the amendment to insert "bake sale" before "fundraiser." If adopted, the main motion will read "to host a bake sale fundraiser this summer." All those in favor please say "aye."

Some: Aye

Chair: All those opposed please say "no." (*Silence*) The ayes have it and the motion is amended. The question is on the motion to host a bakesale fundraiser. Is there any discussion?

Commit or Refer

The motion to commit or refer sends the pending motion to a **committee**, a smaller group of people subordinate to the larger deliberative body, for research and recommendations. A *motion to recommit* is made if the assembly wishes to send the motion to a committee for a second time. Some characteristics of the motion to commit or refer are:

- It requires a second.
- It is debatable.
- It is amendable,
- It requires a majority vote for adoption.

There are two types of committees. A **standing committee** is a permanent committee that is named in the deliberative body's constitution or bylaws. These committees will be discussed more in Chapter 11. For example, let's pretend a local charity is considering a motion "to create a scholarship named after the late Dolores Savannah."

> **Dr. C:** I believe Ms. Savannah has done amazing things for the community and deserves to have a scholarship named in her honor. The Scholarship Committee should conduct research and create qualifications for the scholarship before we have a final vote on the motion. I move to refer the motion to the Scholarship Committee.

A **special committee** is a temporary committee that is created by the motion to commit or refer. The maker of the motion should specify how many members are in the committee and how the members are selected. This selection can be by naming, electing, or appointing.

> **Mr. A:** I move to refer the motion to a special committee consisting of Mr. A, Ms. B, and Prof. Q.
>
> OR

> **Mr. A:** I move to commit the motion to a special committee of 3 people elected by the entire membership.
>
> OR
>
> **Mr. A:** I move to refer the motion to a special committee of 5 people appointed by the President.

If the first example is adopted, the three people would be members of the special committee should they choose to accept their nomination. After the second example is adopted, the body would then nominate different people and vote on who they want to be on the committee. If the third is adopted, the president would then proceed to appoint the individuals to the committee.

The presiding officer of a committee is called a **chairman**. Standing committees elect their chairman. In the case of special committees, the chairman is chosen depending on the appointing authority. The committee chairman of a special committee is the first person named in the motion or the first person the presiding officer appoints. In the case of electing members, the body that elects committee members also has the authority to elect the committee's chairman.

The motion to commit or refer can also be made with or without instructions. These instructions tell the committee how to operate. The committee has to follow these instructions. Instructions can include when the committee is to meet, when it should report, how it should consider the motion, and whether it should hire an expert consultant. Committees can also be granted "full power" to act on behalf of the deliberative body. This includes the ability to spend money or add more members.

Dr. C: I move to refer the motion to the Scholarship Committee with instructions to report back at our next regular meeting.

Postpone to a Certain Time

The motion to postpone to a certain time puts off a motion until a certain time, meeting, or event. Some characteristics of the motion to postpone to a certain time are:

- It requires a second.
- It is debatable.
- It is amendable.
- It requires a majority vote for adoption.
- It requires a 2/3 vote if it makes the postponed question a special order.

The postponed question becomes an order of the day. There are two types of orders of the day: general orders and special orders.

For the following examples, a local school board is considering a motion "to build a library at PS 128."

Prof. X wants to postpone the motion until the next meeting.

Prof. X: I move to postpone the motion to next meeting.

Judge Y wants to postpone the motion until a certain time during the meeting.

Hon. Y: I move to postpone the motion until 8:30 PM.

Principal Z feels like this motion will be debated for a while. He wants the motion to be considered after the special vocal performance.

> **Mr. Z:** I move to postpone the motion until after the musical selection of PS 127.

The above examples of the motion to postpone to a certain time create a general order. Each requires a majority vote. For the first example, the motion would be considered at the next meeting after unfinished business but before new business. In the second example, the motion would be considered at 8:30 PM if and only if there is no business pending. If there is pending business at 8:30 PM, then the motion would be considered after the business is concluded. In the last example, the motion would come up after the musical selection. If general orders are made for the same time, they are disposed of in the order they were made.

For the following examples, delegates to a national convention are considering a motion "to set the salary of the National Director to $50,000." This is the first day of a five day convention.

Since more delegates are attending tomorrow, Mrs. Truman believes everyone should have the opportunity to discuss this important motion.

> **Del. T:** I move that the motion be postponed to the next meeting and be made a special order.

Mr. Ulysses believes the motion should be considered after the convention's lunch hour, no matter what.

> **Del. U:** I move that the motion be postponed and be made a special order for 1:00 PM.

The above examples of the motion to postpone to a certain time create a special order. Each requires a 2/3 vote. For the first example, the motion would be postponed until the next meeting and would be considered before unfinished business. With the second example, the motion would be postponed until 1:00 PM. At that point, it would interrupt any pending business. Special orders interrupt any pending business except 1) adjournment or recess; 2) questions of privilege; and 3) special orders made *before* the current special order.

Let's pretend that the convention adopted Mr. Ulysses's motion and that the time is 1:00 PM.

> **Chair:** The time is now 1:00 PM. A special order was made to consider a motion at this time. The question is on the motion "to set the salary of the National Director to $50,000." Is there any discussion?

Limit or Extend Debate

The motion to limit or extend debate sets/changes the limits of debate for a pending motion or a series of pending motions. Some characteristics of this motion are:

- It requires a second.

- It *not* debatable.

- It is amendable (and the amendments are not debatable).

- It requires a 2/3 vote for adoption.

This motion can *limit* debate by setting the number or length of speeches.

> **Mr. A:** I move to limit debate on the motion to ten minutes.
>
> OR

> **Mr. A:** I move to limit debate on the motion to 1 speech per speaker.

It can also specify at what time debate should close and the pending question should be put.

> **Mr. A:** I move that at 4:00 PM debate be closed and the question on the motion be put.

It can *extend* debate by allowing longer or more speeches.

> **Mr. A:** I move to extend Dr. C's time to 6 minutes.

Forms of the motion to limit or extend debate can also be combined to one motion. If a motion to limit or extend debate is adopted, the presiding officer should appoint a member to keep time.

> **Mr. A:** I move that debate be limited to one speech per person with debate closing at 2:30 PM and all pending questions being put. (*Second*)

> **Chair:** It has been moved and seconded to limit debate to one speech per person with debate closing at 2:30 PM and all pending questions being put. This motion is not debatable but would anyone like to offer an amendment? (*Silence*) Are you ready for the question? (*Silence*) The question is on the motion to limit debate. All those in favor please rise. [*Counts*] Thank you, be seated. All those opposed please rise. [*Counts*] Thank you, be seated. Two-thirds have risen in favor so the motion is adopted. The chair appoints Ms. B to be timekeeper.

Previous Question

The motion to the previous question stops debate and amendment of one or more pending motions and brings them directly to a vote. Some characteristics of this motion are:

- It requires a second.
- It is *not* debatable.
- It is *not* amendable.
- It requires a 2/3 vote for adoption.

Let's pretend that a High School's Band Parent Association is considering a motion "to purchase new brass instruments." There is an amendment "to strike out 'new' and insert 'used' " and a motion to refer to the Ways and Means Committee pending. The association is debating the motion to refer.

Mr. A: I move the previous question.

Mr. A's motion to the previous question is in its simplest form. This motion would end debate and amendment of the immediately pending question, the motion to refer.

Ms. B: I move the previous question on the motions to refer and amend.

Ms. B's motion, if adopted, would end debate and amendment of the motion to refer and motion to amend. If you wish to move the previous question on more than one motion, you must start with the most recent motion and go in order; you can't skip around. Let's look at Dr. C:

Dr. C: I move the previous question on the motion to refer and the main motion.

Chair: I'm sorry Dr. C but your motion is out of order. The previous question can only be applied to motions consecutively.

The presiding officer has to be careful when putting the question on this motion since the name "previous question" can be confusing to new members and new scholars of parliamentary procedure.

Rev. D:I move the previous question on all pending motions. (*Second*)

Chair: It is moved and seconded to order the previous question on all pending motions. For clarification, this motion would end the debate and amendment on all pending questions. All those in favor please rise. [*Counts*] Thank you, be seated. All those opposed please rise. [*Counts*] Thank you, be seated. Two-thirds have risen in favor so the motion is adopted. The question is on the motion to refer.

Mr. A: (*Interrupts*) Mr. President, I move to amend the motion by striking out "Ways and Means" and inserting "Music." (*Second*)

Chair: I'm sorry Mr. A but your motion is out of order. Debate and amendment is closed on all pending questions. The question is on the motion to refer. All those in favor say "aye."

Some: Aye

Chair: All those opposed say "no."

Some: No

Chair: The noes have it, and the motion is not adopted. The question is on the motion to amend. If this motion is adopted, the main motion will read "to purchase used brass instruments." All those I favor please say "aye."

Some: Aye

Chair: All those opposed please say "no." (*Silence*) The ayes have it and the motion is carried. The question is on the main motion "to purchase used brass instruments." All those in favor please say "aye."

Some: Aye

Chair: All those opposed please say "no."

Some: No

Chair: The ayes have it, and the motion is adopted.

Lay on the Table

The motion to lay on the table is the last subsidiary motion. The purpose of this motion is to *temporarily* set something aside when an emergency event pops up. Some characteristics of this motion are:

- It requires a second.

- It *not* debatable (but the presiding officer can ask the maker to state his reason).

- It is *not* amendable.

- It requires a majority vote for adoption.

This motion should not be confused with the motion to postpone indefinitely. The motion to lay on the table is used only to temporarily set aside business, not to kill anything.

For example, a local charity is considering a motion "to donate $100 dollars to hurricane relief efforts." There is also a scheduled guest speaker.

Mr. A: I move to table the motion.

Chair: What is your purpose for tabling the motion?

Mr. A: Our guest speaker has to catch the early train out of town so we should let him speak first then take care of business.

Ms. B: [*Rises*] I second the motion.

Chair: It is moved and seconded to table the motion. All those in favor say "aye."

Some: Aye

Chair: All those opposed please say "no." (*Silence*) The ayes have it, and the motion is tabled. The Chair recognizes Mr. A to introduce our guest speaker for the morning.

To consider something laid on the table, a motion to take from the table is required. This will be discussed in Chapter 6.

4
Privileged Motions and Rank

The second type of secondary motions is privileged motion. **Privileged motions** are motions that do not relate to the business at hand but to special matters of immediate importance. They include the motions to: call for the orders of the day, raise a question of privilege, recess, and adjourn.

Call for the Orders of the Day

The motion to call for the orders of the day is a request by a single member for the deliberative body to stick to its general orders, special orders, agenda, etc. Some characteristics of this motion are:

- It can interrupt a speaker.
- It is a request by a single member.
- It does *not* require a second.
- It is *not* amendable.

- It is *not* debatable.

If the presiding officer is doing his job of announcing the items of business, it is unneeded to call for the orders of the day. However, the presiding officer can make a mistake sometimes by skipping over an item of business or not noticing when a special or general order is to take place.

After the order has been called for and disposed of, the meeting resumes back to the business it was considering.

For the following examples, a homeowner's association is considering a motion "to approve the construction of a neighborhood well." At the last meeting, a motion "to appoint Cindy Jackson to be Neighborhood Manager" was postponed to be a special order for 4:00 PM at the next meeting. The time is now 4:00PM.

> **Dr. C:** This well will provide cleaner, cheaper water to all members of our neighborhood.
>
> **Mr. A:** [*Rises*] I call for the orders of the day.
>
> **Chair:** The orders of the day have been called for. At last meeting the association postponed the appointment of Cindy Jackson to this meeting at 4:00 PM and made it a special order. Since it is now 4:00 PM, the question is on the motion "to appoint Cindy Jackson to be Neighborhood Manager."
>
> [Debate and consideration of the motion]
>
> **Chair:** The ayes have it, and Ms. Jackson is appointed Neighborhood Manager. When the orders of the day were called for, we were considering the motion "to approve the construction of a neighborhood well." At that time, Dr. C had the floor. Dr. C, you may continue

your remarks.

Calling for the orders of the day does not require a vote. However, a 2/3 vote in the negative can stop proceeding to the order.

> **Mr. A:** [*Rises*] I call for the orders of the day.

> **Chair:** The orders of the day have been called for. At last meeting the association postponed the appointment of Cindy Jackson to this meeting at 4:00 PM and made it a special order.

> **Ms. B:** I object. I believe the business we're considering right now is more important than the order.

> **Chair:** The question is: Will the association proceed to the orders of the day? All those in favor please rise. [*Counts*] Thank you, be seated. All those opposed please rise. [*Counts*] Thank you, be seated. Two-thirds have *not* risen in favor so the call fails. The question is on the motion concerning the construction of the well.

Raise a Question of Privilege

A question of privilege relates to the rights of the deliberative body or its members. It is an immediate request that deals with comfort or reputation. Some characteristics of this motion are:

- It can interrupt a speaker.
- It is a request by a single member.
- It does, *not* require a second.
- It is *not* amendable.
- It is *not* debatable,
- The presiding officer rules on it.

Questions of privilege relating to the rights of

the entire body include heating, ventilation, lighting, noise, and other disturbances.

> (During debate)
>
> **Mr. A:** We should adopt this motion because it is very beneficial to...
>
> **Ms. B:** (*Interrupts*) We can't hear Mr. A's remarks in the back!
>
> **Chair:** Mr. A, can you please talk louder into the microphone?

Questions of privilege relating to the rights of a member include the dignity of the individual.

> (During debate)
>
> **Mr. A:** At our last meeting, Ms. B said that she would rather sit on a porcupine than donate another penny to the charity fund.
>
> **Ms. B:** (*Interrupts*) Mr. President, he is misstating my remarks, and I take offense to what he said.
>
> **Chair:** Mr. A, please apologize to Ms. B and sit down.

Since raising a question of privilege can interrupt a speaker, the presiding officer must decide on whether or not it is urgent enough to temporarily set aside business to consider the question.

> **Mr. A:** Mr. President, if we don't close the windows by noon, the amount of light in here will be unbearable.
>
> **Chair:** Thank you, Mr. A. However, since it is only 9:00 AM right now, we will deal with the windows closer to noon.

Recess

A motion to recess is a motion to take a temporary break. It is a privileged motion when there is business pending before the deliberative body. Some characteristics of this motion are:

- It requires a second.

- It is *not* debatable.

- It is amendable (and the amendments are not debatable).

- It requires a majority vote for adoption.

This motion must include a time, duration, or event to specify how long the break is to last.

Dr. C: I move to recess until 3 PM.

OR

Dr. C: I move to recess for 15 minutes

OR

Dr. C: I move to recess until the ballots have been counted.

After the motion has been adopted, the deliberative body takes a break. When it is time to return to business, the presiding officer calls the meeting back to order.

Chair: The meeting will come to order. The time for recess has expired. The question is on the motion "to purchase accounting software for the Treasurer." Is there any discussion?

Adjourn

The motion to adjourn closes the meeting. It is a privileged motion if there is business pending before the deliberative body. The business that it interrupts will be resumed at the next scheduled meeting during the time for unfinished business. Some characteristics of this motion are:

- It requires a second.
- It is *not* debatable.
- It is *not* amendable.
- It requires a majority vote for adoption.

Although the motion is not debatable, it is in order to inform members of business that requires attention before adjournment, make important announcements, and make a motion to reconsider a previous vote. The motion to reconsider will be discussed in Chapter 6.

> **Mr. A:** I move to adjourn. (*Second*)
>
> **Chair:** It has been moved and seconded to adjourn. All those in favor say "aye."
>
> Some: Aye
>
> **Chair:** All those opposed say "no." (*Silence*) The ayes have it and the meeting is adjourned.

Order of Precedence

The 11 subsidiary and privileged motions talked about so far fall in a certain order. The **order of precedence** is a ranking of motions that dictate when a motion is in order. In Chapters 3 and 4 we learned the order of the motions from lowest rank to highest. Let's take a look at the chart on the next page.

Order of Precedence

Adjourn	Privileged
Recess	
Raise a Question of Privilege	
Call for the Orders of the Day	
Lay on the Table	Subsidiary
Previous Question	
Limit or Extend Debate	
Postpone to a Certain Time	
Commit/Refer	
Amend	
Postpone Indefinitely	
Main Motion	

The order of precedence starts with privileged motions being of highest rank followed by the lower ranked subsidiary motion to the lowest ranked main motion. Secondary motions are applied *during* the consideration of a main motion.

If a secondary motion of higher rank is pending, one of lower rank cannot be made. There are two exceptions though: 1) if a motion is amendable, the motion to amend can be made and 2) if a motion is debatable, a motion to limit/extend debate can be made.

For example, an executive board of directors is considering a main motion "to reimburse the President's travel expenses."

Mr. A: I move to refer the motion to a special committee of three appointed by the president. (*Second*)

Chair: It has been moved and seconded to refer the motion to a special committee of three appointed by the president. Is there any debate? [*Sees Ms. B's hand raised*] [1] Ms. B

Ms. B: I move to amend the main motion by inserting "50% of" before "the."

Chair: That motion is out of order because it is of lower rank than the motion to refer. [*Sees Dr. C's hand*] Dr. C

Dr. C: I move to amend the motion to refer by striking out "president" and inserting "board." (*Second*)

Chair: It has been moved and seconded to amend the motion to refer by striking out "president" and inserting "board." Is there any discussion?

Ms. B: Parliamentary inquiry[2], Mr. President. How come Dr. C's motion to amend was in order but my motion wasn't?

Chair: The motion to refer is being applied to the main motion. A motion to amend the main motion is of lower rank than the motion to refer; therefore, it was not in order. Dr. C's motion to amend was being applied to the motion to refer. Since the motion to refer is amendable his motion was in order.

1: Board procedure is discussed in Chapter 11

2: Discussed in Chapter 5

5
Incidental Motions

The third and final type of secondary motions is incidental motions. **Incidental motions** are questions or requests that deal with procedure. They include points of order, appeals, parliamentary inquiries, points of information, dividing the question, dividing the assembly, and withdrawing motions.

Point of Order

A point of order is raised by a member when he feels like a rule has been violated. It is the presiding officer's responsibility to enforce the rules; however, every member has a right to insist on the enforcement of rules. Some characteristics of this motion are:

- It does *not* require a second.
- The maker may interrupt the speaker if the point is urgent.
- It is *not* debatable.

- It is *not* amendable.

- The presiding officer rules on the point.

Let's pretend a community improvement board of trustees is considering a motion "to erect five water fountains at the local park."

> **Mrs. E:** I move to amend the motion by inserting "and purchase a copy of Robert's Rules of Order for the chairman" after "park."
>
> **Chair:** Is there a second?
>
> **Dr. C:** Point of order, Mr. Chairman. Mrs. E's amendment is not germane.
>
> **Chair:** Your point is taken well, and the amendment is out of order. The question is on the motion to erect five water fountains. Is there any discussion?

Appeal

Sometimes a member may not agree with the presiding officer's ruling on a point of order. Any two members have the right to appeal the presiding officer's decision and let the deliberative body decide. Some characteristics of an appeal are:

- It requires a second.

- It is debatable with exceptions- No member may speak more than once and the presiding officer may speak first defending his ruling and last rebutting statements said during debate.

- It is *not* amendable.

- It requires a majority *or* tie vote to sustain the chair's decision.

Mr. A: I move the previous question. (*Second*)

Chair: It is moved and seconded to order the previous question. For clarification, this motion would end the debate and amendment on the pending motion. Is there any debate? Mr. A

Ms. B: Point of order, Mr. President. The motion to the previous question is not debatable.

Chair: Ms. B, your point is not well taken. The assembly will discuss on whether it wishes to end debate or not.

Ms. B: I appeal the decision of the chair. (*Second*)

Chair: It has been moved and seconded to appeal the decision of the chair. Is there any discussion? (*Silence*) Hearing none, the question is: "Shall the chair's decision stand as the decision of the assembly?" All those in favor, say "aye." All those opposed, say "no."

Some: No

Chair: The noes have it and the chair's decision is overruled. [Conducts vote on previous question]

Parliamentary Inquiry

Members have the right to actively participate in meetings. Knowing parliamentary procedure is one way to make sure your voice is heard. If a member has a question about parliamentary procedure, he can ask a parliamentary inquiry to get an answer. Some characteristics of a parliamentary inquiry are:

- It does *not* require a second.
- The maker may interrupt the speaker if the question is urgent.
- It is *not* debatable.
- It is *not* amendable.

- The presiding officer answers the question.

The answer to a parliamentary inquiry is simply an <u>opinion</u> of the presiding officer. Since it is not a ruling or decision, it is not subject to an appeal. The presiding officer is not obligated to answer hypothetical questions.

> **Mr. A:** I move to refer the motion to the Finance Committee. (*Second*)
>
> **Chair:** It has been moved and seconded to refer the pending motion to the Finance Committee. Is there any debate?
>
> **Ms. B:** Parliamentary inquiry, Mr. President.
>
> **Chair:** Ms. B
>
> **Ms. B:** What vote is required to adopt a motion to refer?
>
> **Chair:** A majority vote is required.

Point of Information

A point of information is much like a parliamentary inquiry in the way that they ask questions. A point of information asks questions concerning the current business, but not about parliamentary procedure. Some characteristics of a point of information are:

- It does *not* require a second.
- The maker may interrupt the speaker if the point is urgent.
- It is *not* debatable.
- It is *not* amendable.
- The presiding officer answers the question or directs a member/officer to answer it.

For example, a local charity is considering a motion "to reestablish the hurricane relief fund."

Dr. C: Point of information, Mr. Chairman.

Chair: What is your question?

Dr. C: Why was the relief fund abolished in the first place?

Chair: Mrs. E, you are the former director of the fund. Can you answer Dr. C's question?

Mrs. E: Certainly. [Answers question]

Division of a Question

When there is a motion relating to a single subject but contains several parts, the deliberative body may consider the several parts as if they were separate motions by adopting a motion for the division of a question. Some characteristics of this motion are:

- It requires a second.

- It is *not* debatable.

- It is amendable.

- It requires a majority vote for adoption.

This motion has to clarify how the question is to be divided.

Mr. A: I move to thank our guest speaker by purchasing a card that can be signed by the members. (*Second*)

Chair: It is moved and seconded "to thank our guest speaker by purchasing a card that can be signed by the members." Is there any debate?

Ms. B: [*Rises*] Mr. President

Chair: Ms. B

Ms. B: I move to divide the motion by first voting on thanking the guest speaker and then voting on the card purchase. (*Second*)

Chair: It is moved and seconded to divide the motion- the first part relating to thanking the guest speaker and the second part relating to the card purchase. Are you ready for the question? (*Silence*) The question is on the motion to divide. All those in favor say "aye."

Some: Aye

Chair: All those opposed say "no." (*Silence*) The ayes have it, and the motion is adopted. The question is on the first part of the divided motion "to thank our guest speaker." Is there any debate?

The presiding officer would then put the question on the second part of the divided motion. In order for a motion to be divisible, each part must be able to stand as an independent question and not rely on another part of the motion.

Ms. B: I move to refer the motion to the Finance Committee with instructions to report back at our next regular meeting. (*Second*)

Chair: It is moved and seconded to refer the pending motion to the Finance Committee with instructions to report back at our next regular meeting. Is there any debate? Dr. C

Dr. C: [*Rises*] I move to divide the question so that we can take a separate vote on the instructions.

Chair: I'm sorry, Dr. C, but this motion is not divisible. If the motion to refer with instructions were to be divided into two parts, one concerning the committee and the other concerning the instructions, and the part concerning the committee failed, considering the part concerning the instructions would be pointless. The second part is dependent upon the first.

Division of the Assembly

Motions that require a majority vote should first be voted on with a voice vote. However, any single member can object to this vote and have it verified by a rising vote by calling for a division of the assembly. Some characteristics of a division are:

- It does *not* require a second.
- It is *not* debatable.
- It is *not* amendable.
- A single member demands a division, and it must be carried out.

A single member can demand a division after a voice vote is announced by the presiding officer. This can be done without recognition by the chair.

Chair: The ayes have it and...

Mr. A: (*Interrupts*) Division!

OR

Mr. A: I call for a division

The presiding officer then proceeds to have the revote.

Chair: A division is called for. All those in favor of the motion please rise. [*Counts*] Thank you, be seated. All those opposed please rise. [*Counts*] Thank you, be seated. The ayes have it, and the motion is adopted.

Withdrawing a Motion

A member can sometimes make a poorly-worded motion or a motion without much thought. A member can ask permission to withdraw his motion from the assembly. There are two scenarios in which this can happen:

The first scenario is when a member wishes to withdraw his motion *before* the presiding officer has restated it to the deliberative body. Any member has the right to withdraw his motion before the presiding officer has restated it. When the presiding officer states the motion before the body, the motion becomes the property of the body, not the maker of the motion.

> **Ms. B:** I withdraw my motion.
>
> **Chair:** Ms. B's motion is withdrawn.

The second scenario occurs *after* the presiding officer has restated the motion to the deliberative body. The maker of the motion then has to ask permission for his motion to be withdrawn. Permission is granted only if the entire body agrees. If a single member objects, the presiding officer puts the question.

> **Ms. B:** I ask permission to withdraw my motion.
>
> **Chair:** Is there any objection? (*Silence*) Without objection, Ms. B's motion is withdrawn.
>
> OR
>
> **Chair:** Is there any objection?
>
> **Dr. C:** I object!
>
> **Chair:** There is an objection. The question Is: Shall the motion be withdrawn?
>
> [Conducts vote. A majority is needed]

6

Revival Motions

There is one final type of motion. **Revival motions** bring a motion back for the deliberative body to consider again. Revival motions include the motions to: take from the table, rescind, discharge, and reconsider.

Take from the Table

A motion to take from the table is the opposite of a motion to lay on the table. After the urgent event has taken place, a member seeks recognition from the presiding officer and makes this motion. Some characteristics of this motion are:

- It requires a second.
- It is *not* debatable.
- It is *not* amendable.
- It requires a majority vote for adoption.

This motion must be made during the same meeting or by the next meeting something was laid on the table. If not, business on the table dies.

Mr. A: I move to take from the table the motion concerning the donation to the Hurricane Relief Fund. (*Second*)

Chair: It is moved and seconded to take the motion concerning the donation to the Hurricane Relief Fund from the table. All those in favor say "aye."

Some: Aye

Chair: All those opposed say "no." (*Silence*) The ayes have it and the motion is taken from the table. The question is on the motion "to donate $100 dollars to hurricane relief efforts." Is there any discussion?

Rescind

The motion to rescind cancels a previously adopted motion. This motion can apply to any previously adopted motion except for when action has already been taken on the motion itself. Some characteristics of this motion are:

- It requires a second.
- It is debatable.
- It is *not* amendable.
- It requires a majority vote for adoption if previous notice has been given.
- It requires a 2/3 vote if previous notice has *not* been given.

As stated above, there are different conditions for this motion. In order for the motion to rescind to require a majority vote, previous notice must be given. This should be given orally at the previous meeting. A member seeks recognition from the presiding officer either during new business or during announcements.

Dr. C: [*Rises*] Mr. President

Chair: Dr. C

Dr. C: I would like to give notice that I am going to offer a motion "to rescind the creation of the society's library" at our next meeting.

Chair: Thank you, Dr. C. Can you please provide that motion in writing and give it to the secretary? The secretary will then mail a copy of it out with next meeting's notice.

When the secretary gives notice of the next meeting, he will include Dr. C's intent to offer his motion. The secretary's duties are explained in Chapter 9.

At the next meeting

Dr. C: I move to rescind the creation of the society's library. (*Second*)

Chair: It is moved and seconded "to rescind the creation of the society's library." Previous notice of this motion has been given; therefore, it requires a majority vote to adopt. Is there any discussion?

Discharge a Committee

There are times when a deliberative body has referred a motion to a committee and wishes to take the motion out of the committee's hands. If a motion is in the hands of a committee, the body cannot consider a similar motion. Some characteristics of this motion are:

- It requires a second.
- It is debatable.
- It is amendable.
- It requires a majority vote for adoption if

previous notice has been given.

- It requires a 2/3 vote if previous notice has *not* been given.

This motion should only be used if the deliberative body wants to continue without the help of the committee or wishes to drop the matter. If a standing committee is discharged it continues to operate; however, if a special committee is discharged it ceases to exist. Once a motion to discharge is adopted, the deliberative body immediately proceeds to consider the discharged motion.

> **Mrs. E:** I move to discharge the Finance Committee from further consideration of the FY 20__ budget. (*Second*)

> **Chair:** It is moved and seconded to discharge the Finance Committee from further consideration of the FY 20__ budget. Previous notice of this motion was not given so it requires a 2/3 vote to adopt. Is there any debate? (*Silence*) The question is on the motion to discharge. All those in favor, please rise. [*Counts*] Thank you, be seated. All those opposed, please rise. [*Counts*] Thank you, be seated. Two-thirds have risen in favor so the motion is discharged. The question is on the adoption of the FY 20__ budget. Is there any debate?

The motion to discharge can also be combined with a motion to postpone to a certain time. The same vote applies but if it makes a special order it requires a 2/3 vote.

> **Mrs. E:** I move to discharge the Finance Committee from further consideration of the FY 20__ budget and that it be considered after our guest speaker.

Reconsider

Sometimes a deliberative body makes a decision too quickly or ill-advised and needs to reconsider a vote. The motion to reconsider allows bodies to reconsider a vote with some limitations. Some characteristics of this motion are:

- It requires a second.

- It is debatable.

- It is *not* amendable.

- It can *only* be made by a member who voted on the winning side.

- It can *only* be made on the same day the vote was taken.

- It requires a majority vote for adoption.

The reason someone on the winning side can only make a motion to reconsider is to protect its abuse. The winning side means:

- If the motion to be reconsidered was adopted, the people who voted aye.

- If the motion to be reconsidered was rejected, the people who voted no.

The maker of the motion should state how he voted on the motion he wants reconsidered. If a motion to be reconsidered was voted by ballot, a member can waive his secrecy and make this motion.

For example, a board of directors just adopted its annual budget. The treasurer quickly noticed a major error.

Dr. C: (*Rises*) Mr. Chairman

Chair: Yes, Dr. C.

Dr. C: I noticed an error in the budget we just adopted. I move to reconsider the adoption of the budget. (*Second*)

Chair: Dr. C, how did you vote on the motion to adopt the budget?

Dr. C: I voted in favor of the budget.

Chair: Your motion qualifies. It is moved and seconded to "reconsider the adoption of the budget." Is there any discussion? (*Silence*) Are you ready for the question? (*Silence*) The question is on the motion to reconsider the adoption of the budget. All those in favor say "aye."

Some: Aye

Chair: All those opposed say "no." (*Silence*) The ayes have it and the motion to reconsider is adopted. The question is on the adoption of the budget. Is there any discussion?

7
Resolutions

What is a resolution?

A **resolution** is a written main motion. A resolution is used when a motion is complex and needs to be written out or the deliberative body wishes to formally adopt its opinion or feelings on a topic.

The **preamble** is the first part of a resolution that states background information and reasons for adopting the resolution. Each clause begins with "whereas." This is an optional part.

The **enacting clause** is text of the motion. It begins with "*Resolved,* That" then the text of the motion. A period should only appear at the end.

> **Mr. A:** I move to establish a charity fund to help out the city's homeless population.
>
> OR
>
> **Mr. A:** I move to adopt the following resolution:
>
> "*Resolved,* That a charity fund is established to help out the city's homeless population."

Resolutions can also formally state a deliberative body's stance or opinion.

> Whereas, Taxing daycare services increases the cost for adequate childcare;
>
> Whereas, Families with a low income would have to cut daycare from their family expenses; and
>
> Whereas, All children deserve adequate supervision to keep them safe;
>
> *Resolved,* That the Greater Metropolitan Urban League opposes the City Council ordinance establishing a tax on daycare services.
>
> *Rev. Davis*
>
> President[1]
>
> 1: The presiding officer and/or the secretary should sign resolutions and other acts, authenticating that a majority of the membership adopted the resolution's statement.

The presiding officer puts the question on adoption of the resolution just as he would put the question on a main motion.

> **Chair:** The question is on the adoption of the following resolution: [*Reads resolution*] Is there any debate?
>
> OR
>
> **Chair:** The question is on the adoption of the resolution just read. Is there any debate?

If a resolution has more than one enacting clause, it should follow the same format as the preamble.

> Resolved, That...;
>
> *Resolved,* That...; and
>
> Resolved, That...

8

The Presiding Officer

Pat yourself on the back; we've just learned about all the major motions in <u>Robert's Rules of Order</u>. The rest of this guide will talk about the operation of deliberative bodies.

Duties

The **presiding officer** keeps the order of the meeting. Specifically, his duties include:

- Calling the meeting to order (p. 56)
- Announcing the order of business (p. 77)
- Yielding the floor to members to recognize them for debate (p. 10)
- Putting the question (p. 10)
- Announcing vote results (p. 11)
- Enforcing rules of the deliberative body (p. 39)
- Ruling on points of order, subject to an appeal (p. 39)

- Ruling motions out of order (p. 57)
- Responding to parliamentary inquiries (p. 41)
- Enforcing politeness during debate (p. 10)
- Authenticating acts and orders of the assembly (p. 54)
- Announcing the adjournment of a meeting (p. 36)

The presiding officer is referred to as "the chair." This is derived from the Middle Ages when the presiding officer would sit in a chair and the members would set on benches. In meetings, the presiding officer never uses "I" or "me." Instead, he refers to himself as "the chair."

> **Chair:** The chair appoints the following members to the special committee just formed: Mr. A, Ms. B, and Dr. C.

The most common name for a presiding officer is **president**. Boards of directors and committees are normally led by a **chairman**. Legislative bodies prefer the term **speaker**.

Except in a small board or committee (discussed in Chapter 11) the presiding officer should stand when calling the meeting to order, putting a question to vote, ruling on points of order, and announcing the adjournment of a meeting. Other than that, he can sit or stand, whichever is more convenient. This also depends on which is more effective at getting the body's attention to preserve order.

Call to Order

The first thing the presiding officer does is call the meeting to order. At the time the meeting is scheduled to begin, he should look to the audience and see if a quorum is present. If it is, he should rise, rap the gavel lightly, and call the meeting to order.

> **Chair:** A quorum being present, this meeting will be in order. [*Raps gavel*]

Impartiality

The presiding officer should be impartial. He shouldn't take one side or the other on a motion. During debate, he should make every effort to see that each side is equally heard.

> **Chair:** There have been a few speakers in favor of this motion; is there anyone opposed who wishes to speak?

The presiding officer cannot publicly vote, because that ruins his impartiality. He may vote by ballot or if his vote breaks/creates a tie.

Helpfulness

The presiding officer shouldn't be so technical that he doesn't assist members with parliamentary procedure. He can help members form motions.

> **Rev. D:**[*Rises*] I think we should close debate. [*Sits*]
>
> **Chair:** Do you move to close debate?
>
> **Rev. D:**[*Nods head*]
>
> **Chair:** Rev. D moves the previous question. Is there a second?

Dilatory Motions

Sometimes members want to abuse

parliamentary procedure by continuing to make dilatory motions. A **dilatory motion** is a motion made with the intent of delaying business. The presiding officer should rule these out of order. If a majority of the membership believes it is a legitimate motion, they may seek to appeal the presiding officer's decision.

> **Ms. B:** I move to postpone the motion until February 31.

> **Chair:** I'm sorry Ms. B but your motion is out of order as February 31 does not exist.

Temporary Presiding Officers

Since the presiding officer is most likely a member of the deliberative body, he has the same rights as every member. If he wishes to debate a motion, he must relinquish the chair and allow another member to preside. Debating a motion would ruin the impartiality of the presiding officer.

The *vice-president* (or *vice-chairman* or *speaker pro tempore*) presides when presiding officer relinquishes the chair. He presides over the meeting until the consideration of the motion is over. He then returns the chair to the regular presiding officer.

If the deliberative body doesn't elect a vice-president, vice-chairman, or speaker pro tempore, the presiding officer has the authority to appoint another member to temporarily preside. This is subject to a majority vote, if ordered.

If the presiding officer isn't available to call the meeting to order, the deliberative body's secretary should call the meeting to order and preside over electing a temporary chairman.

9
The Secretary and Minutes

In addition to the presiding officer, the other necessary officer for a meeting is the secretary. The **secretary** (also known as a **clerk** or **scribe**) writes minutes.

Duties

In addition to writing the minutes, the secretary has other administrative duties. Specifically, his duties include:

- Writing the minutes (p. 61)
- Recordkeeping (p. 60)
- Notifying members of their appointment to committees or election to offices (p. 60)
- Giving committees the papers they are to consider (p. 60)
- Sending out meeting notices (p. 60)
- Attesting acts and orders of the assembly (p. 54)

Recordkeeping

The secretary is the custodian of the deliberative body's records (unless the bylaws specify another individual). He should keep on file all committee reports, a membership roll, current copy of the bylaws, standing rules, and minutes. These should be organized in a record book and brought to every meeting. A member has the right to review the record book at a reasonable time and place. This right should not be used to annoy the secretary.

Notifying

The secretary is also responsible for notifying members of their appointment or election to offices, committees, or delegate selection. This can be a written letter, an email, phone message, etc.

He should also notify members of meetings by issuing the *notice of a meeting*. This can be mailed or sent electronically to all members to notify when the next meeting is taking place. In the notice, the secretary should also include members' previous notice of offering motions to rescind, discharge a committee, etc. It should also include any general and special orders postponed to the meeting.

Committee Organization

If a motion is referred to a committee, the secretary should give a copy of the motion to the chairman and a list of instructions (if any). If a special committee is made, the secretary should notify the members of their appointment and also provide them with a membership roster.

Minutes

Minutes are a record of what business was transacted at the meeting. They should focus on what was done, *not* what was said. Minutes should also be free from the secretary's personal thoughts on what happened during the meeting.

The minutes should include:

- All main motions and revival motions (except for ones withdrawn)
- All secondary motions (except for ones defeated or withdrawn)
- The final text of main motions or how they were disposed of (referral to a committee, tabled, etc.)
- Notices of revival and other motions
- All points of order with the presiding officer's ruling
- Important announcements

The minutes should *not* include:

- The person who seconded motions
- Entire text of written reports
- Summary of guest speaker's remarks (just include the name of the speaker and the subject of the speech)

The first paragraph of the minutes should entail the name of the deliberative body; date and location of the meeting; who called the meeting to order and at what time; and if the minutes of the previous meeting were approved.

Central High School Investment Club Minutes
January 15, 20__

A meeting of the Central High School Investment Club was held in Rm. 323 on January 15, 20__. President Grace Day called the meeting to order at 2:10 PM. The minutes of the last meeting were approved as read.

The club received the Vice President's report. The report is filed with the minutes.

The Treasurer's report showed a balance of $300. The report was filed for audit.

The Membership Committee reported the club's two new members: Chuck Baggerly and Clara Chan.

Alejandro Lopez moved "to host a school-wide stock market competition." After debate, Clara Chan moved to table the motion in order to hear the guest speaker's remarks. The motion was tabled.

Mary Christiansen, President of the Central Area Investment Firm, spoke about teenagers accessing the stock market.

After Mrs. Christiansen's speech, the motion concerning the stock market competition was taken from the table. Erik Auburn moved "to refer the motion to the Program Committee with instructions to report back at our next meeting." The motion to refer was adopted and the main motion was referred.

Ken Udeshi, Fundraising Committee Chairman, announced that signup sheets for the club's bake sale will be circulated at the end of the meeting.

The meeting was adjourned at 3:00 PM. The next meeting is scheduled for January 22, 20__.

Adam Kurk

Secretary

10

Treasurer and Officer Reports

Treasurer

The **treasurer** (also known as a **bookkeeper**) is the chief financial officer of a deliberative body. He is responsible for the receipt and disbursement of money and for filing any local, state, or federal taxes.

At each meeting, during officer reports, the treasurer should give a brief summary stating total receipts, expenditures, and account balance. The full report is then filed for audit. That means, just like the minutes, the financial report can be viewed at a later date for more details.

> **Chair:** Mr. Treasurer, can you please give the financial report?
>
> **Mr. T:** Mr. President, our total receipts are $1,000 and our total disbursements are $400. The total balance as of March 20__ is $600.
>
> **Chair:** The report will be filed for audit.

The report is filed for audit, because not all

members are able to do quick mental math to verify the accuracy of the treasurer's report.

Financial Report for March 20__

Receipts

February 20__ balance	$400
Membership Dues (2 new members)	$200
Donations	$400
Total Receipts	$1000

Disbursements

Postage	$100
Office Support	$200
Bank Fees	$100
Total Disbursements	$400

Total Balance:	$600

Timothy T. Truman

Treasurer

The financial reports should be audited annually by an independent auditing firm or an auditing committee of the body. The treasurer then prepares an annual report which is formally adopted by a majority vote.

Officer Reports

Other officers of deliberative bodies may submit reports. These are periodic reports that detail what the member has done in his capacity as an officer. They are read then filed with the minutes. Periodic reports will be discussed more in Chapter 11.

11
Boards and Committees

A **committee** is a smaller group subordinate to a larger deliberative body. A board is small if it has no more than about a dozen members. Committees and small boards should follow less formal procedures, including:

- Members do not have to stand up and address the chairman to speak. They may raise their hand to get recognition and speak from their seats.

- Motions do not have to be seconded.

- Motions to close and limit debate generally shouldn't be in order.

- The chairman doesn't have to stand when putting questions to a vote.

- The chairman may speak in debate and make motions without leaving the chair. (In committees, the chairman should be the most active participant.)

Boards

Boards are an administrative body of elected or appointed people. They set policy and act on behalf of the general membership between meetings. Boards only have the powers that are delegated by the deliberative body's bylaws or organizational documents. A board cannot delegate tasks to other bodies. Instead, it can appoint committees to do its work and report back, subject to the board's approval.

Boards should also take minutes of their meetings. They also present an annual report to the general membership. This report details the activities the board accomplished during the year.

Committees

Meetings of committees are called by its chairman. If the chairman fails to call a meeting, any two members may send notice for a meeting. The quorum for committee meetings is set in the bylaws. If not, it is usually a majority of the membership.

A **standing committee** is a permanent committee that is named in the deliberative body's constitution or bylaws. A **special committee** is a temporary committee that is created by the motion to commit or refer. Special committees cease to exist after the task referred to them is complete.

Reports

Boards and committees can only report what a majority of the members agreed to. If the vote is close and there is a strong minority, these reports can contain a *minority report,* or the views of those who did not vote with the majority. There are two types of reports: annual/periodic and business reports. These reports can be written or verbal. Committees and boards select a reporting member, the person who is to read the report and make any motions related to it.

Annual/Periodic Reports

These reports are generally for information only and summarize work done by the board, committee, or officer. At the end, annual/periodic reports can also contain any recommendations for the deliberative body to implement. This is done by a motion "to implement the report's recommendations" which requires a majority vote to adopt.

Written reports are long and detailed. The reporting member reads the report to the assembly. The minutes should not include the full text of officer reports; however, the full report should be placed on file with the minutes.

Chair: Do any officers wish to report? Mr. Vice President.

Ms. V: [Reads report]

"**Report of the Vice President**
The Vice President wishes to report the following:

1) I attended the recent area luncheon on behalf of the charity and received multiple contacts for future donors.

2) Through our persistence, our County has incorporated a Drop Everything and Read Day to the schools' calendar.

Valerie Valor

Vice President"

Verbal reports are quick, to-the-point reports. The secretary can summarize these reports in the minutes as a written copy is not available for filing.

> **Chair:** The chair recognizes Brother John, Fraternity Membership Committee Chairman, for a report.
>
> **Bro. J:** The membership committee reports that all qualified pledges were initiated last night and recommends purchasing pins for all new members. I move to implement the committee's recommendation.
>
> **Chair:** The question is on the implementation of the committee's recommendation. Is there any discussion?

You will notice that Brother John's motion did not require a second. That is because the motion was made on behalf of a committee. Since committees consist of more than one person, the two person requirement (mover and seconder) is met.

Business Reports

When a motion or resolution is referred to a committee, the committee reports back its recommendations through a business report. Recommendations can range from adoption, rejection, amending, or other parliamentary actions.

> **Mr. A:** The Ways and Means Committee was referred the motion "to purchase a copy of Robert's Rules of Order for each officer" and recommends the adoption of the motion.
>
> **Chair:** The question is on the motion "to purchase a copy of Robert's Rules of Order for each officer." The Ways and Means Committee recommended adopting the motion. Is there any discussion?

Since the presiding officer cannot restate motions made in the negative, he must be careful when putting the question on a motion that has a negative recommendation.

> **Chair:** The question is on the motion "to purchase a copy of Robert's Rules of Order for each officer." The Ways and Means Committee recommended not adopting the motion. Is there any discussion?

If a committee cannot muster up a majority vote to have a recommendation of adoption or rejection, it can report that it has "no recommendation."

A committee can also recommend amendments to motions and resolutions. The presiding officer should put the question on the amendment first, then the main motion.

> **Ms. B:** The Beautification Committee was referred the following resolution: "*Resolved,* That the Homeowners Association construct a water fountain." The committee recommends the resolution be amended by inserting "in the front of the neighborhood by the welcome sign" at the end. We also recommend that the resolution be adopted, as amended. I move to adopt the amendment.

> **Chair:** The question is on the motion to amend the resolution by inserting "in the front of the neighborhood by the welcome sign" at the end. If adopted, the resolution will read "*Resolved,* That the Homeowners Association construct a water fountain in the front of the neighborhood by the welcome sign." The Beautification Committee recommends the adoption of the amendment. Is there any discussion?

Committees can also recommend different parliamentary actions for the deliberative body. It is handled in a very similar way as other recommendations.

> **Dr. C:** The special committee which was referred the motion "to construct a life-sized gold statue of the chapter president," recommends that the motion be postponed indefinitely. On behalf of the committee, I move to postpone the motion indefinitely.

> **Chair:** The question is on the motion to postpone indefinitely. Is there any discussion?

Recommendations for parliamentary actions can range from postponement to referring the motion to another committee.

Hearings

In addition to meetings where committee members debate and research referred items, hearings offer additional information that is valuable to the work of the committee. **Hearings** are forums held by committees where members of the full deliberative body can come and present their views on an issue pending before the committee. Committees should hold hearings if they are considering very important items of business.

12
Voting

Voting is the most important thing a member of a deliberative body can do. The results of a vote set the will of the entire deliberative body. Deliberative bodies use different styles of voting depending upon the situation.

Majority Vote

A **majority vote** is more than half of the votes cast. Most motions require a majority vote. When counting a majority vote, you should *not* include abstentions. An **abstention** is when a member does not vote.

For example, if there were 78 members present at a meeting and only 40 members voted, a majority vote (more than 20) would be 21 votes.

2/3 Vote

A **2/3 vote** means at least two-thirds of the votes cast. When calculating a 2/3 vote, do *not* include abstentions. For example, if 60 votes were cast, a 2/3 vote (at least 40) is 40 votes. If 61 votes were cast, a 2/3 vote (at least 40.66667) is 41 votes. An easy way to calculate this is to multiply the number by 2 then divide by 3.

Motions that require a 2/3 vote are special because they take away rights of members. For example, the motion to limit debate takes away the right to debate and the motion to discharge takes away the right for a committee to deliberate.

Voice Vote

The most common method of voting is a voice vote. **Voice votes** (also known as **viva voce** or **acclamation**) occur when the presiding officer asks those in favor of the motion to say "aye" and those opposed to the motion to say "no." The louder side wins. At the conclusion of the vote, the presiding officer announces the winning side.

> **Chair:** All those in favor of the motion say "aye."
>
> **Some:** Aye
>
> **Chair:** All those opposed, say "no."
>
> **Some:** No
>
> **Chair:** The ayes have it, and the motion is agreed to.
>
> OR
>
> **Chair:** The noes have it, and the motion fails.

Rising Vote

A **rising vote** occurs when the presiding officer asks for each side to rise when called upon. This provides for a more accurate account of how many people are for or against the motion. Motions requiring a 2/3 vote are always conducted by a standing vote.

Chair: All those in favor of the motion please rise. [*Counts the number of people*] Thank you, be seated. All those opposed to the motion please rise. [*Counts the number of people*] Thank you, be seated. The ayes have it, and the motion is adopted.

OR

Chair: The noes have it, and the motion fails.

A member cannot request a division of the assembly on a rising vote. If he wants the vote to be further verified, he can make a motion "to have the vote counted" which requires a majority vote.

Ballot Vote

A **ballot vote** is conducted when the motion at hand requires secrecy. Ballot votes occur when required by the deliberative body's bylaws or ordered by a majority vote.

The presiding officer appoints tellers to conduct a ballot vote. Tellers distribute the ballots, collect them, count them, and report the results to the presiding officer. The presiding officer can always vote by ballot since ballot votes are secret and won't ruin his impartiality.

Chair: The chair appoints Rev. D and Mrs. E to be tellers on this vote. The slips of paper are being distributed. If you are in favor of the motion, please write "yes." If you are opposed, please write "no." When you are done marking your ballot, please raise your hand and a teller will collect it.

[Vote is conducted.]

Chair: Do any members still wish to vote? (*Silence*) Hearing none, the polls are closed. The tellers will count the ballots. The meeting will be in recess until the results are announced.

When counting ballots, the tellers should put to the side any blank ballots or abstentions since they are not counted when calculating a majority or 2/3 vote. Next, they count the number of votes cast and mark that number down. Then, the tellers should count the number of "yes" votes and "no" votes and mark those numbers down. Finally, the tellers count the illegal votes.

Small technical errors, like the misspelling of a word, do not make a vote illegal if the meaning of a ballot is clear. Illegal votes are unintelligible ballots or ballots cast for an unidentifiable candidate. They are still used when calculating the number of votes cast, which is used to calculate how many votes are needed for a majority or 2/3 vote.

The tellers take the numbers they wrote down and write up a small report that is handed to the presiding officer.

Tellers Report

Number of votes cast..45
Necessary for adoption (majority)..................................23
Votes in favor..32
Votes against...10
Illegal Votes
One ballot containing "yes" and "no", rejected................1
Two ballots drawn with a smiley face, rejected................2

The presiding officer reads the tellers report before the deliberative body and announces the result of the vote. The tellers report is entered in full in the minutes. After the completion of a ballot vote, if there is no possibility the body may order a recount, the ballots may be destroyed.

Voting Provisions

Even though all members with an opinion should vote, every member still has the right to abstain because he cannot be compelled to vote. Members can also partially abstain if the motion requires multiple answers (such as electing five people to a committee).

A member cannot explain his vote during voting, because that is considered debate. When a vote is being conducted, debate is closed.

Any member has the right to change his vote up until the vote is announced. After that, he must ask unanimous consent to change his vote.

Unanimous Consent

Unanimous consent occurs when every member at a meeting agrees with an action. It is used to expedite business of the deliberative body.

[During debate]

Mr. A: It seems here a lot of members are interested in seeing this researched some more before we take a vote on it. I ask unanimous consent to refer the pending motion to the Ways and Means Committee.

Chair: Is there any objection? Hearing none, the motion is referred.

If a single member objects, the unanimous consent is lost. The member should then put the unanimous consent request in the form of a motion.

Ms. B: I ask unanimous consent to recess the meeting for 5 minutes.

Chair: Is there any objection?

> **Dr. C:** I object.
>
> **Chair:** This is an objection.
>
> **Ms. B:** I move to recess for 5 minutes.

The presiding officer also has the power to initiate unanimous consent requests.

> **Chair:** If there is no objection, the motion relating to the establishment of a society library will be taken from the table. (*Pauses*) Hearing none, the motion is taken from the table. The question is on the motion "to establish a library for the society." Is there any discussion?

13

Order of Business

The **order of business** is the sequence of which business should be taken up. Some deliberative bodies adopt their own order of business. <u>Robert's Rules of Order</u> recommends the following standard order of business:

    I. Reading and Approval of Minutes

    II. Reports from Officers, Boards, and Standing Committees

    III. Reports from Special Committees

    IV. Special Orders

    V. Unfinished Business and General Orders

    VI. New Business

The presiding officer announces each heading before the deliberative body begins to consider business under the heading.

Reading and Approval of Minutes

At the beginning of every meeting, the presiding officer should call upon the secretary to read the minutes of the previous meeting. This reading can be waived if all members are furnished with a copy of the minutes.

> **Chair:** The first order of business is reading and approval of minutes. Mr. Secretary, can you please read the minutes of the previous meeting.
>
> **Sec:**   [*Reads minutes*]

After the reading is complete, the presiding officer then asks for any corrections to the minutes. Here, members can make motions to amend the minutes. This is usually done by unanimous consent. The presiding officer then puts the question on approving the minutes, which is also generally done by unanimous consent.

> **Chair:** Are there any corrections to the minutes? Hearing none, the minutes stand approved as read.

After the minutes have been approved, the secretary initials them and writes "approved."

Reports from Officers, Boards, and Standing Committees

Under this heading, the presiding officer recognizes officers, boards, and standing committees for their reports. Here, they can give their annual/periodic reports or their business reports. These reports are discussed in Chapter 11.

> **Chair:** The next order of business is reports from officers, boards, and standing committees. The chair recognizes Professor Q, Chairman of the Ways and Means Committee, for the committee report.

Reports from Special Committees

This heading is the same as Reports from Officers, Boards, and Standing Committees except for the presiding officer calls upon special committees.

Special Orders

Under Special Orders, the presiding officer calls up items of business that have been made a special order for the meeting. If the special order does state a time, it is considered generally under this heading. If any special orders were left unfinished from last meeting, they are considered under this heading.

> **Chair:** The next order of business is special orders. At last meeting, a motion relating to the location of our annual meeting was postponed to this meeting and made a special order. The question is on the motion "to have our annual meeting at the City Resort." Is there any discussion?

Unfinished Business and General Orders

If a meeting adjourns before it finished considering all of its business, it becomes unfinished business for the next meeting. Under this heading, unfinished business and general orders are considered. Also, things laid on the table but not taken up from last meeting can be considered. General orders are created by a form of the motion to postpone. The presiding officer doesn't ask for any unfinished business, he simply states it and consideration begins.

> **Chair:** The next order of business is unfinished business and general orders. The unfinished business is the

motion "to allocate funds for the delegates' expenses to the National Conference." Is there any discussion?

New Business

Under new business, members make motions and offer resolutions.

> **Chair:** The next order of business is new business. Do any members wish to make a motion?

Agenda

The presiding officer can make an unofficial agenda to keep the business organized. Under each heading, it should include any items known in advance that will be considered at the meeting. The presiding officer should contact all committee chairmen and officers to ask if they have a report. If any members tell him in advance of a motion they want to offer, he should put it on the agenda and give them preference when calling on members to offer motions.

> Sample Agenda
> 1. Call to Order
> 2. Approval of Minutes
> 3. Officer Reports
>   a. Vice President
> 4. Committee Reports
>   a. Ways and Means
>   b. Membership
> 5. Unfinished Business
>   a. Picking location of annual meeting
> 6. New Business
>   a. Mr. A's motion to set date of group picture

14
Conclusion

You did it! In under 100 pages we learned all the basics of parliamentary procedure! Take the knowledge you studied from this book back to your club, civic organization, charity, etc and help other members be more aware of what happens at meetings. You should be truly proud of yourself. If you want to study more parliamentary procedure, I suggest you either buy more of my books in the future or pick up the latest edition of Robert's Rules of Order Newly Revised at your nearest bookstore. After a few miscellaneous items, a glossary, and index, you are finished with this book. Pat yourself on the back and walk into your next business meeting with a sense of pride.

Glossary

Abstention: When a member doest not vote.

Articles of Incorporation: A legal document that gives the name and object of an association.

Ballot vote: Type of vote used when the motion at hand requires secrecy.

Boards: Administrative body of elected or appointed people.

Bookkeeper: *See "Treasurer"*

Bylaws: *See "Constitution"*

Chairman: *See "Presiding officer"*

Clerk: *See "Secretary"*

Committee: A smaller group of people subordinate to the larger deliberative body.

Constitution: Document that contains the organization's basic rules.

Conventions: An assembly of delegates who are representatives from constituent local chapters.

Deliberative body: A group of people that use parliamentary procedure to make decisions.

Dilatory motion: A motion made with the intent of delaying business.

Enacting clause: The text of the motion in a resolution.

Germane: Relating to the pending motion in some way.

Hearings: Forums held by committees where members of the full deliberative body can come and present their views on an issue pending before the committee.

Incidental motions: Questions or requests that deal with procedure.

Legislative bodies: Constitutionally mandated lawmaking bodies for the general public.

Local Chapters: Groups of people who belong to a bigger parent organization who wish to meet on a more frequent basis with other members who live geographically close to each other.

Main motion: A motion that brings business before the deliberative body.

Majority vote: More than half of the votes cast.

Mass Meetings: Large assemblies of people.

Minutes: A record of what business was transacted at the meeting.

Motion: A proposal.

Order of business: The sequence of which business should be taken up.

Order of precedence: A ranking of motions that dictate when a motion is in order.

Parliamentary Law: *See "Parliamentary procedure"*

Parliamentary procedure: A set of rules, customs, and ethics that guide the governance of clubs, organizations, and other deliberative bodies.

President: *See "Presiding officer"*

Presiding officer: Officer who keeps the order of the meeting.

Primary amendment: An amendment to a motion.

Privileged motions: Motions that do not relate to the business at hand but to special matters of immediate importance.

Putting the question: When the presiding officer puts the motion up for a vote.

Quorum: The minimum number of people that must be present in order for business to be transacted.

Resolution: A written main motion.

Revival motions: Motions that bring a motion back for the deliberative body to consider again.

Rising vote: When the presiding officer asks for each side to rise when called upon

Rules of Order: The set of parliamentary procedures that an organization adopts.

Secondary amendment: An amendment to an amendment.

Secondary motion: A motion that relates to a main motion by procedural or emergency qualities.

Seconder: The person who agrees a motion should be considered.

Secretary: Officer who writes minutes.

Speaker: The name many legislative bodies choose for their presiding officer.

Special committee: A temporary committee that is created by the motion to commit or refer.

Standing committee: A permanent committee that is named in the deliberative body's constitution or bylaws.

Standing Rules: Additions to the rules of order the organization has already adopted.

Subsidiary motions: Motions that help dispose of a main motion.

Treasurer: The chief financial officer of a deliberative body.

2/3 vote: At least two-thirds of the votes cast.

Unanimous consent: When every member at a meeting agrees with an action.

Viva voce: *See "Voice votes"*

Voice votes: When the presiding officer asks those in favor of the motion to say "aye" and those opposed to the motion to say "no."

Index

K

L

M

N

O

P

www.ingramcontent.com/pod-product-compliance
Lightning Source LLC
Chambersburg PA
CBHW062045280526
45788CB00003B/1121